WHEN
TRAGEDY
STRIKES

CHARLES STANLEY

THOMAS NELSON PUBLISHERS®
Nashville

A Division of Thomas Nelson, Inc.
www.ThomasNelson.com

Published in Nashville, Tennessee, by Thomas Nelson, Inc.

Unless otherwise indicated, Scripture quotations are taken from THE NEW AMERICAN STANDARD BIBLE ®, Copyright © The Lockman Foundation™ 1960, 1962, 1963, 1968, 1971, 1972, 1973, 1975, 1977. Used by permission. (www.Lockman.org)

Scripture quotations noted NIV are taken from the HOLY BIBLE, NEW INTERNATIONAL VERSION®. Copyright© 1973, 1978, 1984 by International Bible Society. Used by permission of Zondervan Bible Publishing House. All rights reserved.

The "NIV" and "New International Version" trademarks are registered in the United States Patent and Trademark Office by International Bible Society. Use of either trademark requires the permission of International Bible Society

Library of Congress Cataloging-in-Publication Data

Stanley, Charles F.
    When tragedy strikes / Charles Stanley.— [Rev. ed.].
    p. cm.
    ISBN 0-7852-6121-4 (hardcover)
    1. Suffering—Religious aspects—Christianity. 2. Consolation. I. Title.
BV4905.3.S73 2003
248.8'6—dc21

                          2003017495

Printed in the United States of America

03 04 05 06 07 PHX 5 4 3 2 1

Contents

Foreword   vii

1. When Tragedy Strikes   1

2. Compassion and Concern   15

3. Becoming a Comforter   25

4. We Need Each Other   35

5. Living Fearlessly   41

6. God Is in Control   51

7. Forgiveness: A Way Out   61

8. Discovering the Good:
   A Divine Boundary   69

Conclusion   91

About the Author   96

Psalm 27:1–3

The LORD is my light and my salvation;
   Whom shall I fear?
The LORD is the defense of my life;
   Whom shall I dread?
When evildoers came upon me to devour
   my flesh,
My adversaries and my enemies,
   they stumbled and fell.
Though a host encamp against me,
   My heart will not fear;
Though war arise against me,
   In spite of this I shall be confident.

Foreword

I am writing this book some time after our nation experienced the devastation of the terrorist attacks on September 11, 2001. Since then, I have had opportunity to consider, prayerfully, the impact of those events on our nation, and I have come to realize that to the citizens of America, the toll of this national calamity is essentially a representation of what happens day by day in the lives of millions of individuals across the globe who face tragic events that consume their lives, their time, and their energies.

The truth is, however, that when disaster strikes a person, it is almost impossible for that experience to be merely an individual matter. Usually loved ones at home, parents, siblings, extended families, and friends and neighbors are affected and involved.

Bearing this in mind, I want us to consider together some of the issues that inevitably manifest themselves when tragedy strikes us. With God's help, we will see that without living in fear, we can, to some degree, be prepared so that when tragedy suddenly comes our way, we may have some understanding as to what we should do and how we should respond to the crisis. Our source for guidance in this matter will be God's Word. It has much to say about dark and difficult days and how we should respond to them.

As we reflect together, I am going to refer to the 9/11 situation not only because it is still a very vivid memory for all of us, but also because out of the horror of those days there are some lessons to be learned about dealing with tragic events. For example, individual and group responses to the disaster were so helpful to the bereaved and to many of the survivors, enabling them to get through their pain and anguish.

Also, I want to point out that the "best" in human beings is often demonstrated when tragedy strikes. People from all walks of life provided the finest examples of what we can do and how we can help grieving and suffering people.

Finally, all of us need to be reminded that our God can and does bring good from evil—even in the midst of unthinkable horror. He is present to help and give us His blessed comfort. My prayer for every reader of this book is that you will see very clearly God's perspective regarding tragic events, and if now or in the future you face critical hours or days, you will know He desires to intertwine your needs with His wonderful understanding and help you to "go on" and "get through."

1

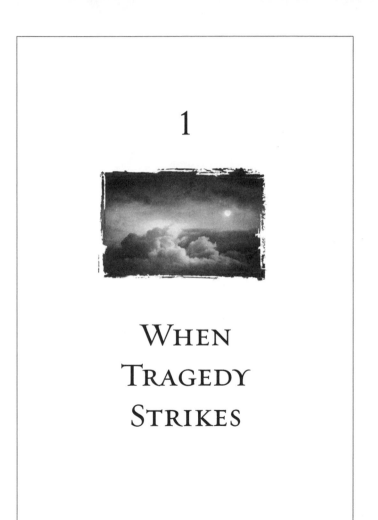

WHEN
TRAGEDY
STRIKES

Hidden away on the third page of our newspaper in mid-November 2001, was the story of thirteen miners who died at the Blue Creek No. 5 mine in Brookwood, Alabama. Apparently there was an initial explosion, and three miners were trapped, injured, or killed. Ten other miners immediately went into the mine to try and rescue their stricken colleagues. While seeking their friends to give them aid, another explosion occurred, and all thirteen men lost their lives.

And do you recall some years ago when a little child in Texas fell into a well and the ensuing struggle by paramedics and firefighters to find and rescue her? If I remember correctly, the child was trapped for almost twenty-four hours, and the longer the event wore on, the more focused the nation became on that little one. The life-and-death concerns around that child grabbed America's attention, and millions were riveted to the TV, until finally she was rescued safe and sound, except for some bruises and a lot of tears. It was as though all of us had participated in the event, and we all shared the thrills when she was saved.

I suppose these stories would have grabbed front-page headlines on a "normal" day, but the days immediately following 9/11 were anything but normal.

It seems to me that because of the 9/11 attacks, as never before in our lifetime, many of us Americans feel we are now living in a world where the possibility of death and disaster loom as very real causes for concern. Intuitively, we seem to understand that the enormity of the disaster that ensued as a result of the attacks in New York and Washington, D.C., makes other tragic moments in the day-to-day affairs of our nation pale in comparison. Yet, we all know that the heartache stemming from any type of tragedy is very real, and no matter how small or localized the circumstance, it affects deeply all of those who are involved. So, we dare not make light of any situation that leaves people in grief.

The pain and sorrow caused by tragic circumstances affect all cultures and societies. Sooner or later, every person will be faced with the sadness and difficulties associated with a sudden traumatic event that will change forever life as they know it. And tragedy comes in different shapes and sizes. Individuals, families, cities, regions, and nations experience horrifying disasters. And, as in the case of the attacks on the World Trade Center and the Pentagon, some tragic events affect the entire world.

In recent memory we recall massive damaging earthquakes in Turkey and Mexico that took many lives. We shudder at the thought of hundreds killed in religious warfare in Northern Ireland and Indonesia. Some of us remember our sense of disquiet during the days following the nuclear meltdown in Chernobyl. And what can we say regarding the school shootings in Colorado, Oregon, and Kentucky?

Frankly, dear reader, the reality is that tragedies are ever present with us—they are part of our daily existence. But almost always they occur with such devastating abruptness that we are left in shock and panic. We get the phone call about the auto accident. We hear of the heart attack. We catch the quick flash on the evening news about ships colliding on the high seas with the whereabouts of the crew unknown; and much of the time we are stunned by what we see and hear. Sometimes, however, many of us seem to be immune to the sudden news events that should change our status-quo feelings and galvanize us to action but which, in reality, find us sadly apathetic and unmoved by the trauma.

We are children of an age in which tragedy has become part of our daily agenda. Most of the time, tragic events are not something for which we plan. We do not arrange ahead

> TRAGEDIES ARE EVER PRESENT WITH US.

of time to face these sudden crisis moments in our lives, unless, of course, our professional responsibilities direct that we are part of some type of emergency-management team whose specific responsibility is to prepare for such disasters.

Some months ago, I heard an interview with an emergency room physician in Washington, D.C. He described how, in his capacity as chief of disaster preparation for the hospital, the systems he had put into place seemed to work quite adequately as they began bringing in the wounded from the Pentagon attack. Nevertheless, he commented that in spite of all the advance planning, there were many unforeseen situations that became apparent to them as they were flooded with the victims of the disaster. Also, he wondered aloud as to what they would have done if their hospital had been the target of such a terrorist attack.

CHANGED FOREVER

Even the word *tragedy* in our language seems to convey a sense of foreboding and fearful anticipation. So it is no surprise that the events that have happened to our fellow Americans in New York, Washington, D.C., and Pennsylvania in 2001 have stung all of us to the core. We've had many, many different kinds of emotions—disbelief, revenge, rage, frustration, and fear, to name but a few. In my judgment, however, there has been no single historical event since the Civil War that has caused us to recoil with such horror and to view a terrorist attack with so much individual and national anger.

It may well be that our nation will be changed forever. President Bush implied as much when he said, "Our war on terrorism will not end until every terrorist group of global reach has been found, stopped, and defeated," as quoted in *U.S. News and World Report* from October 1, 2001. A terrorist war has come to us, to our own shores. In all the other wars we have taken part in, we have fought to protect our own interests or to help others in their struggles on foreign territory. But now, for the first time, we have been attacked on our own soil—and in such a despicable manner.

This tragedy was the result of a planned, premeditated, clandestine guerilla operation designed to destroy the lives of thousands of innocent people. Hate and bigotry motivated it, and, worst of all, it was cloaked in religious fervor. That fact alone makes it horrific!

This was the evil work of evil men whose minds were darkened to the point of believing that they could indiscriminately maim and murder thousands of people and be rewarded by their god. These were actions stemming from depraved minds, minds with no sense of shame or conscience, that purposed to create mayhem and havoc in America by destroying thousands of innocent people.

It did not take our leaders and the nation as a whole much time to see clearly that these terrorists' actions represented an act of war against our country. I doubt, however, that the internal emotions and passions felt on 9/11 by people across our nation and those who lost loved ones are different from those feelings experienced by someone whose loved one was killed recently in an accident caused by a drunken driver or in a random shooting. In other words, those parents whose children lost their lives in the Columbine shootings have experienced the same grief and sorrow as those who lost family and friends on 9/11. The impact of the sudden implosion in their lives is the same.

The fact is we are residents of planet Earth and live with others in various cultural, societal, and economic circumstances. As a result, all of us are candidates at some time or another for an unforeseen crisis to occur in our lives and, although it is impossible to really be prepared, there are things we should know and understand that will, in those moments, enable us to survive and even thrive despite the tragedies we may face.

THE LORD IS THE DEFENSE
OF MY LIFE

Some of us are old enough to recall how difficult it can be to live through a period when the nation is at war—facing an enemy seeking to destroy all that we hold sacred and dear. In such times people seek and need help, comfort, assurance, and safety. I am convinced that there is no better place to turn than to our God who has promised to help those who call upon Him in times of trouble. Yes, faith in an unseen yet very present God is the foundation for inner peace no matter what the crisis we face. In the time of trouble, it is the opportune moment for us to look up and seek our God and to ask Him for words of comfort and strength for our hearts.

Many of God's saints have known trouble and difficulty as they journeyed through life. Consider David, the psalmist of Israel. Though he was anointed and chosen to be king, he found himself hated and hunted by those who sought to destroy him. In Psalm 27, however, notice what he says while in the midst of trouble:

> The LORD is my light and my salvation;
>> Whom shall I fear?
> The LORD is the defense of my life;
>> Whom shall I dread?
> When evildoers came upon
>> me to devour my flesh,
> My adversaries and my enemies,
>> they stumbled and fell.
> Though a host encamp against me,
>> My heart will not fear;
> Though war arise against me,
>> In spite of this I shall be confident. (vv. 1–3)

These are the words of a man who had learned how to be sustained in the most difficult, trying times of life. He learned an amazing lesson—in the midst of imminent danger and possible attacks on his person and family, he did not need to live in fear, because God was his defense. Though in a war zone, he could be fully confident that God would protect and sustain him.

Like King David, there is hope for us too, because God has promised never to leave us or to forsake us. And we can have confidence in the future, because we are not alone—we have each other. As individuals and a nation, this must be our strength—a united spirit gaining assurance and determination from each other while we continue to trust in and rely on our God.

2

COMPASSION
AND
CONCERN

How should we respond when, like a bolt out of the blue, our cherished ideals, the safety of our families, our future security, and all the other dreams of life for which we have labored and invested much time and effort are suddenly threatened? As I pondered and prayed about this question, it became clear to me that there are some answers.

First, if you are the victim, you must remember that you are not alone. Even if family and friends for some reason cannot gather around you to share your grief, listen to your pain-filled words, and dry your tears, you are not forsaken. Our gentle heavenly Father is with you and will compassionately draw near to you and be a "refuge and strength, a very present help in [time of] trouble" (Ps. 46:1). If, on the other hand, we are called to help others in their time of need, we should respond with compassion and concern for them and assure them of a caring "Presence" in their sadness until they are able to move forward with strength.

Compassion and concern can be demonstrated in many ways. Supporting orphaned children through a reputable organization, giving your time and money to help feed and shelter the homeless, and sacrificing your time to help build homes for the needy through Habitat for Humanity are some well-known ways of loving others.

There are times of deep sorrow however, when *you* must be personally involved: A neighbor or close friend suffers a painful loss, or you get a call from a family member telling you that a crisis is occurring in his life, and he needs your help. Of course, you will show your compassion and concern by going to him and being with him. I am sure you will want to do whatever you can to support him in his hour of trial. Over the years of ministry, I have noticed that often the best thing you can do is simply to "be there" for those persons. The assurance of your presence will bring comfort and give them an opportunity to communicate with you if they so choose.

But what does one do when a tragedy of such huge proportions like 9/11 occurs? Do you recall your feelings when you saw those planes fly into the World Trade Center towers? The scenes of people clinging to windows, desperately hoping to escape the inferno engulfing their offices, are still with us. We saw the buildings implode and collapse with thousands of workers and helpers buried beneath the rubble. Can life ever return to normal again? Some people have used the word *surreal* to describe these images, as though they were make-believe scenes from a movie.

How long did it take you to realize that you had entered a new world—one in which things would never be the same for you as an American citizen? Have you been able to give satisfactory explanations to your children about this tragedy? Will the ugly head of post-traumatic stress syndrome manifest itself again as it did after the Vietnam War? How long will it be before the children of those innocent victims display the symptoms that so often accompany sudden tragedies such as this? Yes, we are in the midst of a dark, bleak period in our nation's history—but there is hope, because the answer in this situation is the same as the one where the crisis is localized and occurring in familiar territory and with known friends.

Gordon MacDonald, a pastor and former president of InterVarsity Christian Fellowship, spent a week with the Salvation Army relief teams at the rescue site where the World Trade Center towers collapsed. He and his wife, Gail, worked in horrific conditions from morning to night at "Ground Zero." MacDonald wrote in a letter:

No church service, no church sanctuary, no religiously inspiring service has spoken so deeply into my soul and witnessed to the presence of God as those hours last night at the crash site. In all my years of Christian ministry, as much as I love preaching the Bible and all the other things that I have been privileged to do over the years, being on that street, giving cold water to workmen, praying and weeping with them, listening to their stories was the closest I have ever felt to God. Even though it sounds melodramatic, I kept finding myself saying, "This is the place where Jesus most wants to be."

Friends, when we see God at work through compassionate, caring deeds and when we sense His presence through the caring hands of others, then we can face the future with a degree of confidence that would be utterly lacking and absent from us if we stood alone.

GROUND ZERO

> "THIS IS THE PLACE WHERE JESUS MOST WANTS TO BE."

Soon after the 9/11 tragedy, thousands of workers from all over America were clambering over the debris at the crash site wanting and desperately willing some of those possibly trapped under the rubble to be found and saved. Days after the buildings collapsed, and when most experts believed that there was little hope for finding anyone still alive, these valiant rescuers toiled on, day and night. They had assumed the responsibility of doing what they could. And that is exactly what we are called to do when tragedy strikes our world. In the same manner, we must offer aid, comfort, and compassion to those who have been traumatized—whoever they are, wherever they may be, no matter their race, religion, or status. God calls us to get involved with our comfort and compassion.

Since the advent of television, we are no longer onlookers or passersby: We have become part of ongoing events, players in the action. Remember the child in Texas and the recent hurricane and flood victims in Alabama and Mississippi? Through the medium of TV, we see their dilemma, and we try to imagine what it would be like to suffer as they are suffering. Often we are grateful that we have escaped such loss and pain, but surely it is only the hardened heart that cannot identify with the trauma we see before us. For most people, the television pictures are able to affect us deeply and to ignite compassion in us as we see how others are being affected. This is a good thing. But there must be more; there must be greater roles for us to play than that of being deeply touched by what we see and hear on television. So, what is our responsibility?

3

BECOMING
A COMFORTER

The Word of God makes it very clear that there are certain kinds of people who do best in the arena of becoming a comforter:

> Praise be to the God and Father of our Lord Jesus Christ, the Father of compassion and the God of all comfort, who comforts us in all our troubles, so that we can comfort those in any trouble with the comfort we ourselves have received from God. (2 Cor. 1: 3–4 NIV)

The best comforters are those who have been through trouble and tragedy themselves. They know the feelings, the sadness, and the emotional upheavals that go with the territory. So when we go through adversity, isn't it reassuring to have someone there to walk with us who has endured the same trauma we are experiencing? Especially comforting is to have a friend who reminds us that our God is "the Father of all comfort" who has promised never to leave us or to forsake us.

REACHING OUT

Yes, one of the foundational things we can do in the midst of tragedy is to reach out to people with compassion and understanding—to walk with those in need, to comfort them. People need the loving touch, the embrace of a friend. We need someone to reach out to us in troubling times. Reaching out implies doing something, doesn't it? Compassionate people are those who feel the pain of others, and act to alleviate that pain.

After 9/11, Dr. Bernadine Healy, the then president of the American Red Cross, said:

Everyone is asking "What can I do?" There is much to do in the weeks and months ahead. Reach out to a neighbor, regardless of heritage. Console a grieving friend. Give blood. Volunteer in your community. Make a donation to the charity of your choice. Mostly, sustain this spirit of America at its best. This is a time for compassion.

How right she is. As a pastor, however, I want to ask you to pray and to remember that our greatest source of comfort is God who, through His Son, Jesus, has identified with us in our sorrow and pain. Our Savior was "a man of sorrows and acquainted with grief" (Isa. 53:3). He well understands our situation, our uncertainty, and our fears and through us is able to comfort others.

May I say to you who have picked up this book because you are suffering, God will be your source of comfort and strength. He grieves with you as you bear the awful sense of emptiness and helplessness. He offers you mercy for these dark days. It is His desire to comfort your heart. He is the one "who comforts us in all our affliction" (2 Cor.1:4). It is His nature to comfort His children.

> IT IS HIS NATURE TO COMFORT HIS CHILDREN.

The Scriptures depict God as a loving Father nourishing His children, as a tender, gentle nurse caring for those for whom she is responsible, and as a mother hen hovering over and protecting her chicks. These metaphors are pictures of a God committed to compassionate care for His children.

A fundamental requisite for those who seek to comfort others is the ability to forget about themselves. It is so easy for us to become enamored with our own affairs and to get caught up in our own journeys to significance and success. We must work hard to put others first. Who can ever forget images of Mother Teresa in the suburbs of Calcutta pouring out her life for the poor and needy?

We must become successful comforters by being present while others weep, by sharing our shoulders for others to lean on, and by being reliable and careful listeners. Also, we need to be dependable and trustworthy with the thoughts that are shared with us and avoid giving hasty answers or worn-out clichés to those who grieve. Grieving people need the safety of friends who hold them up, rather than hold them accountable for what they express in anger and frustration. Yes, there is a great opportunity for us to be channels of mercy and comfort in the name of our Lord.

Do you recall my earlier comments about King David? He refused to be ensnared by fear, because he was confident that God was with him and would deliver him from the enemies that pursued him. In Psalm 46 David says, "God is our refuge and strength, a very present help in trouble." This shepherd-boy-turned-king experienced the presence of almighty God in the midst of adversity and tragedy. No matter the circumstance, David's bottom line was his confident assurance that God was present with him!

David's fifty-seventh Psalm has been helpful to me through the years:

Be gracious to me, O God, be gracious to me,
    For my soul takes refuge in You;
And in the shadow of Your wings I will take
        refuge,
    Until destruction passes by. (V. 1)

Perhaps some of you are thinking that, because I am a minister, I have had a life devoid of hardship and tragedy. That would be far from the truth. On many occasions, in the midst of extremely difficult circumstances, I have found myself drawn to that verse as I sought comfort and assurance from God. Here is His promise: When our hearts are so empty and our pain so intense, our hurt so deep and our grief so overwhelming, we are to come to the Father in the shadow of His wings and find a refuge "until destruction passes by."

Mark my words, the destruction, the evil, and the pain will eventually pass! No matter how deeply you hurt, how acute your pain, how hopeless you feel—when you come to your heavenly Father for help and compassion and love, He will be there for you. He will carry you through until you are strong enough to stand alone again.

4

WE NEED
EACH OTHER

Many experts believe that because of the 9/11 hijackings, life and the way we do some things may never be the same again. But of this you can be certain, no matter what transpires to change your circumstances, your heavenly Father will always be the same! He is not thrown by tragedy. The eternal God will walk with you the rest of your life. He will help you to adjust if a new lifestyle is thrust upon you by tragic occurrences; and eventually, He will enable you to understand the "whys" of the tragedy that engulfs you. Further, if you so choose, He will enable you to live life more fully than you have before. As a result of the compassion you receive from others, God will give you the strength to respond to the needs of others with compassion and love.

THE SPIRIT OF COMPASSION

Although some time has passed since September 11, 2001, it still continues to encourage my heart when I see people joining together for the common good. We have been responding passionately and positively to the needs of others. It is a beautiful thing to see, and a beautiful thing in which to share.

I am not surprised to see the American flag flying wherever I go—we are a strong, patriotic nation. Also, I am thrilled to see a spirit of compassion across the nation—compassion in action: people hugging each other, crying on each others' shoulders, and giving a helping hand to one another. For so many, the importance of skin color, language, or heritage has been dramatically erased, and the primary concern of helping others has been taken to heart.

What greater evidence can there be that our nation is a compassionate and caring one than the magnificent example of the 250 fire fighters and police officers who willingly risked their lives to rescue those trapped in the burning towers? They saved the lives of others, but lost their own. The images of the tangled steel ruins are a monument to their devotion to others and to our nation. The permanent memorial planned for the former site of the World Trade Center will be a national symbol to remind all who see it of their compassionate sacrifice.

In spite of some skeptics who choose to downplay the spirit of compassion in America, when I think about what has happened spontaneously all across this country—such as people stepping out of their homes to gather together in communities for candle-lighting ceremonies—clearly a nerve has been touched, an open wound in our national psyche has been uncovered, and we are demonstrating how much we need each other.

For the first time in many a year, we feel emptiness inside, and we are calling out to one another, "Come walk with me . . . let me take your hand . . . do you have time to share this journey?" And some among us have realized the dearth in our souls and they are asking, "How can I get back on track spiritually? Will God hear my prayers? Where do I find spiritual guidance at a time like this?" We have an opportunity to join our hands and hearts together. We are being drawn together in a way that is honorable and affirming.

5

LIVING
FEARLESSLY

We must be courageous to face the tragedies that come our way with a determination to overcome them and to go on living without fear. This doesn't mean that we don't grieve or experience pain. No, we must inevitably taste the bitterness of our losses and dashed hopes. We must endure the pain and keep putting one foot ahead of the other as we struggle to move on with our lives. It doesn't mean we will not have regrets and perhaps, over the years, be confronted with the sudden memories of loved ones gone and the empty holes left in our lives. But we must be encouraged to press on—as our nation is doing right now. Let us all be challenged and encouraged by the courageous spirit we see and sense across the country during these days.

A HERITAGE OF DETERMINATION

As a nation, we are not a fearful people. We do not suddenly give up just because something frightens us. When I was about nine years old, Pearl Harbor was attacked. The American response was unforgettable. Young men, barely sixteen or seventeen years old, lined up to enlist and to serve. They did not care which branch of service would take them; they only wanted to defend their nation.

When united, this country trembles before no other power. We have a national sense of courage and bravery. We have a heritage of firmness and determination that has carried us through many troubling and dangerous times. I want to remind you of this so that none of us will expect anything less of ourselves in our own dark days than what we expect from our nation—a determined, courageous response to the challenges we face.

Doris Dougherty captured this moment accurately when she said, "No greater tragedy can be found than that of a soul crying out 'It's not fair!' and allowing the cold waters of cynicism to overflow and to drown him." She continues that there is no greater victory than to plunge into these waters where the bottom cannot be felt, but the strong person will "swim until I can!" We may not be able to feel the bottom now, but like our nation, we must swim until we do!

In the 1940s America began fighting a war in the Pacific and soon thereafter a war in Europe as well. Back then, America was not heavily industrialized; we were mostly a nation of farmers. We were unprepared for war, and yet we successfully fought on two fronts for four long years. The cost was devastatingly high, but we were triumphant, which says something about our bravery, determination, and national character.

Over these last months, I have seen a new spirit of courage and determination across America. Except for a few people, this has not been an in-your-face, arrogant expression of disdain and self-aggrandizement. On the contrary: It is as if a sleeping giant who has been awakened is confidently taking his rightful position, fully aware of who he is and what he can accomplish. People who have been sitting in the shadows with little interest in joining the game are stepping up to the plate. The spirit of courageous King David has gripped the nation, and we are joining him to boldly assert: "Though a host encamp against me, my heart will not fear. Though war arise against me, in spite of this I shall be confident" (Ps. 27:3).

There may be some reading this book who are fearful, deeply afraid, even overwhelmed, because of the deep psychological wounds from the 9/11 attack. It is not unusual for some of us in any one community to feel bowled over by a moment of significant trauma. I have faced times when the odds seemed totally against me—when the floodwaters were drowning me and my dreams. In moments like that I have recalled a special Scripture that God has used to help me face the floodwaters—the occasions when rational and irrational fears threatened my confidence and contentment. Read this powerful passage:

> Behold, all those who are angered at you
> will be shamed and dishonored; those who

contend with you will be as nothing and will perish. You will seek those who quarrel with you, but will not find them, those who war with you will be as nothing, and non-existent. For I am the LORD your God, who upholds your right hand. (Isa. 41:11–13)

We have a right to be a godly people who are fearless. We have a right to be bold and confident for the simple reason that God has promised to intervene in our behalf. Does that mean that we will never suffer consequences? No, it does not. Will we always be free from hardship and adversity? Of course not. It means that when we, as individuals or as a nation, stand under the protection of our God, then we can be assured that He will not fail us no matter the disaster we face

> WE HAVE A RIGHT TO BE A GODLY PEOPLE WHO ARE FEARLESS.

or the enemy at our gate. With our God we will be triumphant.

We can never know what transpired in the hearts and minds of those men and women who died in the collapse of the World Trade Center buildings, but I am sure that many, knowing that they were about to die, courageously committed themselves into the arms of a loving God—One whose arms were there to shield them from the steel and rubble and usher them gently to their heavenly reward.

There is an old gospel song by Charles Tindley called "Leave It There," that states, "We'll understand it better by and by." Only in eternity will we understand some of the mysterious ways of almighty God. Only then will we grasp the significance of His eternal plan that encompasses all of us.

6

God Is
in Control

We have noted that our responses to tragedy must be made with compassion and concern, and that we must exercise our faith, courage, and confidence in God, who has promised to never leave us or to forsake us. There is another response. It is a natural thing for those faced with sudden calamity to ask, "God, why did you allow this disaster?" We should not ignore this question, but instead face the issue. Many would prefer to leave God out of the discussion, as if they fear that He may have an inadequate response. For those of us who know Him as our heavenly Father, however, we are not afraid to face this issue. We know the clear promises of His

Word, and we know that to seek to understand why God permits tragedy is an appropriate response.

GO AHEAD AND ASK

Some people believe one should never ask questions of God, even though this is not a biblical position. Courageous King David often commented on his inability to understand the ways of God and, at times, was forthright in his probing questions. We can learn the ways of God by seeking answers to difficult problems and heartaches. But we must not leave God out of the equation!

> WE MUST NOT LEAVE GOD OUT OF THE EQUATION!

Consider four types of people who have a difficult time with this issue:

1. *Atheists.* They believe our universe is
    closed, with no possibility of outside
    influence from any source. They believe
    there is no point in introducing God
    into any conversation, because there is
    no such being.

2. *Those who have a warped, distorted
    idea of God.* Inevitably their perceptions
    of God distort His character in some
    flagrant way. For example, they accept
    that He is loving but reject that He is
    a God of holiness and justice. They
    cannot balance these two seemingly
    competing ideas.

3. *Those who have an inadequate
    understanding of Scripture.* Many
    misunderstand the ways of God,
    because they have not studied the

Bible. They question how He acts and why He allows tragedy and evil in this world.

4. *Those who refuse to acknowledge that they are accountable to God.* Unfortunately, many Americans fall into this category. Many are theists who believe in God but choose to live their lives as though He is absent and uninformed about them and their circumstances.

Here are some sobering questions for every category of people, and I use the word *sobering* very deliberately. Did God know about the tragic events that have happened to you before they occurred? Yes, He is omniscient or all-knowing. There is nothing that goes on in our world that the Creator and Sustainer of it does not know. Also, we can say with biblical authority that nothing happens to you or me that He does not allow. Somehow He knows what is ultimately good for us in the grand scheme of His eternal plans.

Did God initiate these events? With issues like the 9/11 attacks we can say categorically, no, but He did permit them to happen. And for some reason, in your particular crisis, although He knew ahead of time about the tragedy that would befall you, He allowed it to happen too. The Scripture says God's throne is established in the heavens and His sovereignty rules over all (see Ps. 103:19). Clearly we are told that God is in charge; He is in control. Nothing happens apart from His knowledge, His understanding, and His power.

If God is not in control, who is? In the tragic circumstances you now face, if God could not have stepped in and stopped it, then somewhere out there is something more powerful than God.

This is not the case, however. Those of us who are believers are convinced by experience and faith that there is no power equal to God in this universe. We believe He is in absolute total control.

If this is true, some will still question, "Why? Why did God allow it to happen?" With all the earnestness in my heart, I respond to you by saying, "You can find out." Please, just ask Him. Prayerfully engage Him with your questions and concerns. He is committed to respond to the open and truthful heart. He is not afraid of your questions. He gives honest answers. As you earnestly and honestly seek Him, I guarantee that He will begin to give you the answers to your questions and, at the same time, start to change and to transform your life. You may even find yourself asking Him: "What do you want to teach me through this series of tragic events?" In my experience God works good out of evil and gives comfort and strength to the most sorrowful heart. That is the kind of God He is.

In one of my books I tell the story of a man who at one particular juncture of his life was distressed by some untruthful accusations that publicly destroyed his character and slandered his reputation. Because of this cruel treatment, his initial response was, "I don't want to live."

God had other plans, however, and in the midst of this heartache, the Lord, in a unique, personal way, whispered to him, "This is My will for you." Believing that God had his best interests at heart and that His heavenly Father was in total control of every facet of his life, he got up from the ground and began to live life to the full. He went from tragedy to triumph because of God's loving concern for him.

7

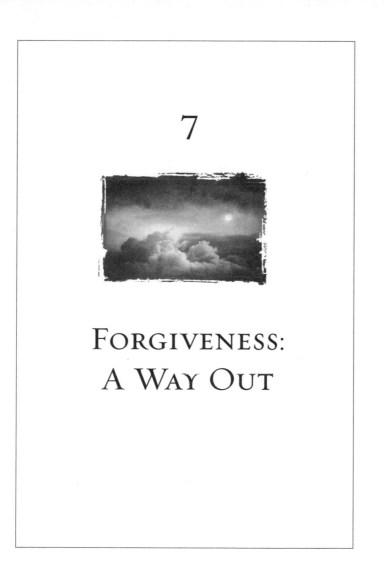

FORGIVENESS:
A WAY OUT

Going from tragedy to triumph almost always requires an act of forgiveness. The man I spoke of in the last chapter, whose reputation was deliberately attacked and destroyed, knew the perpetrator of the crime. He knew that he had been singled out to be falsely accused. With that knowledge, he faced a choice—would he choose the path of forgiveness or elect to remain bitter and antagonistic to the one who had so hurt him? It was a crucial decision.

Thankfully, even as he wept with shame and embarrassment and contemplated what would happen as his family, friends, and associates heard the evil report, the presence of God was so real to him, urging him to lay aside his anger, that without any further ado, he decided since God was involved in the matter with him, he would turn the evil into good. To forgive the offender, then, was a simple matter for my friend. He realized that in failing to forgive, he would not focus on his heavenly Father and His plans for the future, but on the one who was at fault, and it would allow his anger and bitterness to carry the day, with all the consequences that would ensue. Thank God, he made the right choice!

FORGIVENESS IS A CHOICE

Dear reader, there are consequences when we, in a fit of rage, or with a desire for revenge, decide to take matters into our own hands and become an instrument seeking to guarantee a payback on the one who caused our pain and sorrow.

At this juncture, let me remind you again: Forgiveness is a choice. It is something we can do or deliberately decide not to do. Many times, when we are caught up in tragic circumstances, we inevitably want to know why this happened to us, and then we tend to focus on the one who caused our pain. We try to make sense of the matter and often find ourselves rehearsing over and over again the events that transpired to create the havoc we face.

Such times are never easy! Parents who have lost a child through an accident caused by a drunken driver or some other disaster have a right to be angry. They need to express their inner feelings—whatever they are. But if they choose to deal with their pain by not forgiving the one who caused the loss, they eventually will become prisoners of that person and become forever entangled in a disastrous web of accusation, bitterness, negativity, and self-recrimination, which will lead always to a sad, unproductive life.

What, then, is forgiveness?

Forgiveness is the act of setting someone free from an obligation to you that is a result of a wrong done against you. For example, a debt is forgiven when you free your debtor of his obligation to pay back what he owes you.

Forgiveness, then, involves three elements: *injury,* a *debt* resulting from the injury, and a *cancellation of the debt.* All three elements are essential if forgiveness is to take place.

And why is forgiveness so important? Because it is God's chosen means of granting us His mercy in spite of our mistakes and failures. Our Savior was punished in our place. We were forgiven when we did not deserve it. God canceled our debt and forgave us so that we may be rightly related to Him. And this path He chose is the one He insists we must follow. Remember our Lord's Prayer when the disciples said, "Teach us to pray." Our Lord said in Matthew 6:12 that when you pray, ask your heavenly Father to forgive your debts (read "all your failures and the injuries you have caused others") *as you forgive others their sins against you.* He then said, if you will not forgive others, your Father will not forgive you (v. 15).

Friends, just as we choose to love someone, so we can choose to forgive him or her. In that moment of forgiveness, you will begin the process of being healed and made whole. Let me hurriedly say that such an act will not remove the sorrow you feel nor the ongoing loss you experience, but it will make it possible for you to move through your tragic circumstances and eventually get to the other side of your sorrow.

FORGIVENESS
IS THE WAY
OF FREEDOM

In an earlier book, *The Gift of Forgiveness,* I tell something of my own story and the long journey of learning how to forgive those who had severely hurt me. It was not an easy road. Nevertheless, now, by God's grace I am free from any chains of bitterness and antagonism towards others—set free to live in freedom. I assure you, there is nothing better than to know you are forgiven and that you have forgiven everyone who has harmed you in any way. When tragedy strikes, the road through the pain to peace on the other side must be one in which we release all our anger and bitterness toward others and commit them to God. He will judge them justly. Forgiveness is the way of freedom. This is God's way.

8

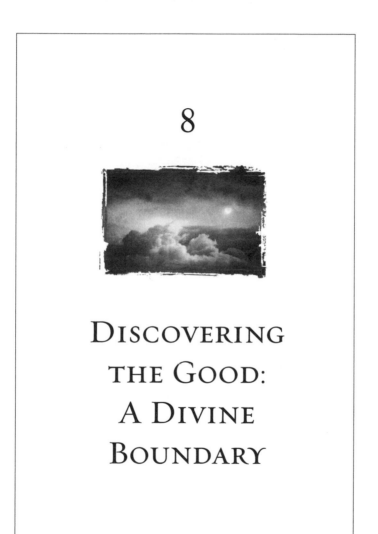

DISCOVERING
THE GOOD:
A DIVINE
BOUNDARY

There's another response that I think is so very important. I believe we are to endeavor to discover the good that God brings from tragic events that threaten us. Some may ask, "How can you even think that anything good could come out of a horrific calamity like the 9/11 attacks?" When we are felled by tragedies, often we are so wounded that even the most ordinary tasks seem gigantic in scope, and the thought that one day things will get back to a degree of normalcy seems incomprehensible.

Deep emotional scarring can blind us to the possibility that in the future there will be healing and peace for even the most traumatized of souls—but healing does come. In fact I know a man in Atlanta who lost two businesses and the love of many of his friends and family, and for years was living in a semipermanent state of depression. Like the phoenix, however, with God's guidance and blessing, he has risen out of the ashes of despair and, with family alongside him, he has become a beacon of hope to many seeking help in the aftermath of personal tragedy. If you asked this man how he was able to rebound, he would probably refer you to Romans 8:28. This is one of the most familiar passages in the entire Bible:

> And we know that God causes all things to work together for good to those who love God, to those who are called according to His purpose.

You may say, "But that refers only to those who love God. What about all these traumatized people who don't love him?" First, why not thank God for the millions of Jesus' followers who do love Him and who represent such a strong stabilizing force in the world? If you do not have a meaningful relationship with Jesus at this time, be grateful that there is a worldwide company of believers—the Church— to pray for, support, and care for you and others like you.

Second, be thankful that God has established limits by which He decrees the boundaries of men's activities. Make no mistake: His purposes and His authority limit the plans of all men. Our Lord has given us freedom of will and choice, to the point where He says, "No further." So, on September 11, 2001, our God allowed and limited the tragedy in New York, Pennsylvania, and Washington, D.C. There was a divine boundary placed upon the events of that day.

In the wake of 9/11, some of us became personally enmeshed within the circle of its devastation, losing relatives and friends, emotional stability, and financial security. Others have been swept up in the aftereffects—the tears, the fears, the losses, and the pain. And this has been the pattern of life, the ebb and flow of good and evil, since the world began—not just since 9/11.

Is there not a balance between freedom and license? Any parent can tell how fraught with danger the pathway to adulthood is for a growing teenager. How much freedom should be allowed? Will his or her necessary struggle for independence and adulthood be too marred by the limits in place for safety and security? These are difficult questions for parents. How much more important is it then for our heavenly Father to exercise His control over the affairs of His world?

LOOK FOR THE GOOD

If it is a good response to a tragedy to look for the good in it, what might we find? Let's look at the aftermath of the 9/11 situation.

1. There has been a greater sense of unity in America than at any time since the second World War. When the twin towers were hit, it seemed almost instantaneously that the nation came together. The nation had been in a crisis of bitterness over a close presidential election, and some thought the delicate balance of political disagreement had vanished into a cauldron of hate, and that the unending bitterness would never stop. Then the terrorist attacks came— and the result? The nation, with all its history of political, religious, and ethnic divisions, came together in a unique way. We were united!

This does not mean, of course, that the ebb and flow of life, whether political or cultural, will not continue to put strain on our sense of national unity. But whatever happens in the future, most of us will never forget that sense of oneness that enveloped America.

2. We have developed a reverence and respect for human life that for many years has been lost in our culture. For example, our nation thrives on competition. We are a sporting nation, and some might even suggest that we have made a god out of sports and of winning at all costs. But in an unthinkable demonstration of respect and reverence for those who lost their lives in New York, Pennsylvania, and Washington, D.C., every major sporting event in our country was canceled for one complete week. Think about the financial losses—the television revenue, the ticket sales, the lost wages, the empty hotel rooms—all considered secondary to the need for the nation to respect human life.

Can you imagine anything that would shut

down a football game or a baseball game, especially during the final series of games to determine the pennant winners? None of us would ever have dreamed that anything could have caused this to happen. The truth is, there was no presidential decree that all sporting events were to be postponed or canceled, as was done by President Jimmy Carter prior to the staging of the Olympic games in Russia in 1980. On the contrary, there was a general consensus that certain activities were no longer appropriate. This attitude speaks of a reverence and a respect for human life that we have not seen for a long time.

3. Also, in my judgment, there was a realization among the general populace that, ultimately, only God can protect our nation. We may search out, round up, incarcerate, and possibly execute those who committed the attacks, but we know that there will always be others ready to take their place. With this in mind, the

vast majority of Americans appeared to want to return to their religious roots. There, to find reassurance that the God of our history, the God of our founding fathers, was present to help and protect the nation.

I am convinced, personally, that only God can protect America. All our armaments, weaponry, financial strength, material resources, and political will cannot guarantee our protection. That is why it is a critical thing for us to turn our hearts back to God.

> ONLY GOD CAN PROTECT AMERICA.

4. For the first time in many, many, decades people have become more important than profit. It is a good thing to see, in this capitalistic society, corporations giving so generously to the needs of others. Millions of dollars have been donated to relief agencies.

The Salvation Army and the American Red

Cross were inundated with gifts for the New Yorkers who suffered such great losses. The Salvation Army had a divisional headquarters on Fourteenth Street in New York City. From the ninth floor, a group of officers with computers and cell phones were continuously locating and distributing food, clothing, and dry goods. From where did these donations come? The generous hearts of Americans. This new, kinder, gentler, and more generous spirit becomes all of us. It says something about the real character of the American people, and it says something good.

5. We have become more God-conscious. Publishers tell us that they sell more books on spiritual and religious subjects in times of crisis than they do during normal circumstances. Do you know why? Because when we find ourselves under duress, when our moorings are adrift, we are unable to provide the internal

self-assurance that things are going to be okay.

Too often, we are incapacitated by feelings of inadequacy and helplessness—that is why we tend to turn to God in difficult times. And this is not a cop-out or the path of someone who is weak and needs a crutch. God has made us in His image and, therefore, we are most alive and whole when we invite Him to nourish and succor us along life's journey. If you are feeling helpless or hopeless right now, here is a great prayer to offer: "Father, you know me best; please help me."

One Sunday morning, I heard an Atlanta radio station comment on the unusual amount of downtown-area traffic confusion. In all the years I have lived in the metro area, I have never heard a traffic reporter state that the reason for the delays was because there were too many people attending church! But that's what he said. May God bless our nation with more and more sensitivity to His presence. Would it not be wonderful if once again His powerful presence would be felt all across our land—in factories, in schools and universities, in corporate offices and state assemblies—wherever people are congregating? May it be so!

6. Another benefit of the crisis, I believe, is that everywhere one went there was a sense of brokenness and grief that blanketed our nation like a cloud. Adults and children alike were affected by the sadness and mourning. Why is this good? Because it has forced many of us to deal honestly with our feelings.

Parents have had an opportunity to communicate with their children, to open doors of understanding and identification. Has your child asked, "Mom and Dad, why were all those people jumping from that building?" "What happens to them after they jump?"

"Dad, would you be okay if you had to jump like that?" "Where would you have gone if you died like that?" "Where did those people go?" Such forthright questions require honest, nonevasive answers.

This has provided a grand opportunity for all of us to deal with the issues of death and dying. We have been forced to face difficult issues, so it has given us an opportunity to consider what types of parents we are. It has given us an occasion for some serious self-evaluation. We have pondered how much time we spend with our families and where they fall on our priority scales.

All across this land there seems to be a new spirit, a new humility, gentility, if you will. This is a good thing that is strongly supported by the bold assertion of Scripture, which says God hates arrogance but loves a broken and a contrite heart.

WHAT LEGACY WILL YOU LEAVE?

I feel there is a greater sense of things eternal than there has been for a long, long time. I saw a man being interviewed whose father was lost in the collapse of the building. In response to one of the questions, he replied, "I am all right because I know where my father is—he is okay." This son was proclaiming for all the world to see and hear that his father had been a Christian and had lived his life so that his son was proud to be known as his son. This man was affirming confidently that although he was grieving and would continue to do so, he would not grieve as one without hope. On the contrary, he was positive that his beloved father was now in the presence of the God he had served so faithfully. The son had been left with a godly heritage. In his pain he was comforted.

What more needs to be said? Since 9/11, we have been given a wonderful opportunity to think not only about the legacy we will leave behind but also about our home for eternity. One of my life's constant concerns relates to the legacy that I will leave my children and grand-children. What have I taught them about life's priorities? Have I lived with integrity? As I have sought to live a life with character, have the posi-tives outweighed the negatives? These questions and a hundred more flood my mind as I think about eternity and how prepared I am to face my heavenly Father.

Dear reader, please take this moment to look at your own life. I have used the 9/11 tragedy to point out how God can bring good from evil. We have considered some of the changes that have affected our nation and how, for the most part, these changes have the marks of divine blessing and encouragement. In the midst of your tragic moments, God can do the same for you—bring good from evil, love instead of hate, a commitment to care for others as never before and a determination not to let the pain of the moment, however long it may be, stop you from becoming a more compassionate, caring human being. If you are in the midst of a dark hour, take comfort and courage from the good that you have seen in your friends and neighbors and, above all, recognize that God is present in your life.

Whatever your need, He is able and will be there for you. In fact, this may be a great time to get serious about your relationship with God. Now is the time to stop driving by church—go in. Get your Bible dirty from fingerprints and tears, rather than letting it be dusty from lack of use. Search for God, and find peace in your soul, rather than seeking for gold and finding poverty in your soul.

A SIMPLE PLAN

SEARCH FOR
GOD, AND
FIND PEACE
IN YOUR
SOUL.

We have discussed how we as individuals should respond to tragic events that come our way. We have considered together how to turn our faces up to God and our hands out to help our fellow man. Finally we must discuss what may be the most beneficial thing to come from any tragedy that crosses our paths—a returning to God's simple, yet profound, plan for our lives.

For some of you, however, there is a fundamental problem with this plan. You feel alienated from God. Frankly, years ago, prior to my becoming a minister, I felt the same way until someone shared with me the good news, the marvelous story of God's eternal plan to help us all reconnect with Him. God created the world through His unprecedented power and authority. He created humans and allowed us to enjoy His beautiful world. But our forefathers messed up, and we have continued to do the same ever since. We rebelled against His principles and laws, and we still do so. In other words—we sin.

Inevitably sin leads us away from God and pushes us to do our own thing. As a result we become more self-reliant and less aware of our need of God. When tragedy comes across our paths, as it always does, we do not have the resources within ourselves to bring peace to our troubled hearts. This is good, because it usually opens a window to our souls, a window that our loving Father can open and use to make contact with us again.

Of course I am talking in generalities, but I do this to show that His plan does include you. No matter how far away from Him you have traveled, He still knows, understands, and loves you. He can open the window to your heart. All that is required is your permission. When you give the word, He will act. Then, you will learn that His Son, Jesus, came into our world to live and to die as one of us, yet still He retained His divinity. Amazing, isn't it? Further, as a sinless man, Jesus was killed because people thought He was a criminal, a fake Christ. Yes, they thought He was an imposter—not the real Son of God. But after His death He did what no other person has ever done: by the power of God, He rose out of death. In doing this He triumphed over it—that nasty reality we all seem to fear. He went back to His Father in heaven and now prays for us and waits to meet us when we die.

There is only one sticking point: God requires us to recognize that we cannot ever be good enough to make it to heaven on our own. Why would Jesus have had to suffer if we could be good enough? No, we are required to ask for His mercy, to confess our sins, and to trust Him for our salvation. That, my friend, is the best piece of good news you will ever hear. I hope that in the center of your tragedy, you will find inner peace and forgiveness. They are the wonderful gifts of God.

CONCLUSION

Since September 11, 2001, the Dow Jones Industrial average has lost more than $1.4 trillion of wealth. Almost all major American airlines have been forced to give pink slips to thousands of workers, and more than eighty of our leading economists now believe we are in a financial recession. Clearly, the effects of 9/11 have touched all areas of our society. Now, as I write, there is conflict in Iraq, and fighting and bloodshed in various countries are daily reminders for all of us that a life without ongoing tragedy is really not possible.

Armed Forces reserve units are being called to active duty, and ships and planes are leaving our shores for unspecified locations for undetermined amounts of time. We are a nation in crisis. This is, however, a grand opportunity for all of us to actively live a life of compassion toward others, to comfort and encourage those who are in dark places of pain and sorrow, to practice a life of offering forgiveness to those who injure us and to renew our faith commitment.

As people of faith, we must maintain our confidence in God so that when we face difficult times, we will have the inner resources to overcome our own personal challenges and, eventually, come through with flying colors. Also, let us mobilize ourselves to steadfastly work and pray for the nation. Now is the time for fervent prayers and ardent patriotism, for passionate giving and selfless living. It is the opportunity of a lifetime to make a change—to be a different person and a different people.

We have an opportunity, by faith, to believe

in each other for a better future; to forgive each other for past wrongs; and to go the extra mile for friend and enemy alike. Out of tragedy can come triumph.

About the Author

D<small>R.</small> C<small>HARLES</small> S<small>TANLEY</small> is pastor of the 15,000-member First Baptist Church in Atlanta, Georgia. He is well-known through his *In Touch* radio and television ministry to thousands internationally and is the author of many books, including *On Holy Ground, Our Unmet Needs, Into His Presence, Enter His Gates, The Source of My Strength, Discover Your Destiny, How to Listen to God,* and *How to Handle Adversity.*

Dr. Stanley received his bachelor of arts degree from the University of Richmond, his bachelor of divinity degree from Southwestern Theological Seminary, and his master's and doctor's degrees from Luther Rice Seminary. He has twice been elected president of the Southern Baptist Convention.

Other Books by Charles Stanley, from Nelson Books

Discover Your Destiny

Enter His Gates

Eternal Security

The Gift of Forgiveness

A Gift of Love

The Glorious Journey

How to Handle Adversity

How to Keep Your Kids on Your Team

How to Listen to God

In Touch with God

Into His Presence

Our Unmet Needs

The Power of the Cross

Seeking His Face

Success God's Way

The Source of My Strength

Winning the War Within

The Wonderful Spirit-Filled Life

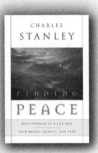